CONNECT

# PRESIDENTIAL POLITICS BY THE NUMBERS

by Mary Hertz Scarbrough

Consultant:
Dennis Showalter, PhD
Professor of History
Colorado College

CAPSTONE PRESS
a capstone imprint

Connect is published by Capstone Press,
1710 Roe Crest Drive, North Mankato, Minnesota 56003
www.capstonepub.com

**Library of Congress Cataloging-in-Publication Data**
Cataloging-in-publication information is on file with the Library of Congress.
978-1-4914-8238-4 (library binding)
978-1-4914-8628-3 (paperback)
978-1-4914-8649-8 (eBook PDF)

**Editorial Credits**
Jennifer Huston, editor; Veronica Scott, designer; Tracy Cummins, media researcher;
Kathy McColley, production specialist

**Photo Credits**
Alamy: SilverScreen, 16 Left; Corbis: 22, Bettmann, 20, Flip Schulke, 26; Flickr:
U.S. Embassy New Delhi, Cover Left; Getty Images: Fox Photos, 18 Right, Hulton
Archive, 13, Lane Turner/The Boston Globe, 18 Left, MANDEL NGAN/AFP, 14,
30, New York Daily News Archive/Dan Farrell, 39, PhotoQuest, 16, 31, Underwood
Archives, 11 Bottom, 29 Bottom, Washington Bureau, 27 Top; JFK Library: White
House Photographs/Cecil W. Stoughton, Cover Right; Library of Congress: 4, 5
Top, 15 (all), 17 Top, 17 Bottom, 23, 24, 25, 29 Top, 34, 35 Left, 38 Top, 38 Bottom,
41 Bottom, 42; Shutterstock: chrupka, 41 Top Right, ducu59us, Design Element,
Everett Historical, 10, 11 Middle, J. Helgason, 11 Top, javarman, Design Element,
Lyudmyla Kharlamova, 5 Bottom, Matthew Cole, 41 Top Left, NatBasil, Design
Element, Nevada31, 27 Bottom, silver tiger, 6–7, 8, 44–45, Vector pro, Design Element,
watcharakun, Design Element; Thinkstock: hermosawave, 28; Wikimedia: 35 Top,
35 Middle, Cecil W. Stoughton, 40, JFK Library, 33, NARA, 9 Bottom, 17 Middle, 32,
National Numismatic Collection, National Museum of American History, 35 Bottom,
Otis Historical Archives Nat'l Museum of Health & Medicine, 36, Robert L. Knudsen,
White House Press Office, 43, U.S. Department of Defense/Eric Draper, 9 Top, United
States government Patent Office, 21, USCapitol, 12

Printed in the United States of America in North Mankato, Minnesota.
032019    001726

# TABLE OF CONTENTS

# CHAPTER 1

# DO THE MATH

Numbers have always played a significant role in characterizing presidents. Sometimes people refer to presidents by their number. For example, George H. W. Bush is often referred to as Bush 41. His son, George W. Bush, is known as Bush 43.

Every president has a number based on how many people have served as president before. George Washington is number 1, of course, since he was the first president of the United States.

**57**

number of presidential elections from 1789 through 2012

**43**

number of men who have been president since 1789

**4**

the greatest number of terms any president has been elected to serve. Franklin D. Roosevelt was elected in 1932, 1936, 1940, and 1944. Because all of his terms were consecutive, he only has one presidential number—32.

**nonconsecutive**—with a gap between; not one after the other

# 2

the number of times Grover Cleveland is counted in the numbering system. He was first elected president in 1884. He ran for re-election in 1888 but lost to Benjamin Harrison. Cleveland won the 1892 election, making him the only president to serve two **nonconsecutive** terms, which is why he is counted twice.

# 22

Grover Cleveland's first presidential number

# 24

Grover Cleveland's second presidential number. If he had been re-elected in 1888, he would only have one number—22—because his terms would have been consecutive.

# $25,000

George Washington's salary when he became president in 1789. That would be about $675,000 in today's money.

# $400,000

President Barack Obama's salary in 2015

# CHAPTER 2

# WHO, WHAT, WHERE: THE ELECTORAL COLLEGI

Unlike a college that you might attend after high school, the Electoral College is not a place. It is how we elect presidents in the United States. Voters cast their **ballots** on Election Day. These results are called the popular vote.

In mid-December, **electors** from each state cast their Electoral College ballots. In most cases, the candidate who wins a state's popular vote gets all the votes from that state's electors. Whoever receives the most electoral votes becomes president. But just getting the most electoral votes isn't enough. In order to become president, the candidate must also receive more than half the total number of electoral votes.

Every state starts with two electors. That's because each state has two senators. Then each state gets additional electors according to the number of members it has in the House of Representatives.

**435** current number of members in the House of Representatives

**100** 50 states x 2 senators for each state

**3** number of electors for the District of Columbia

**538** the total number of electors in the Electoral College

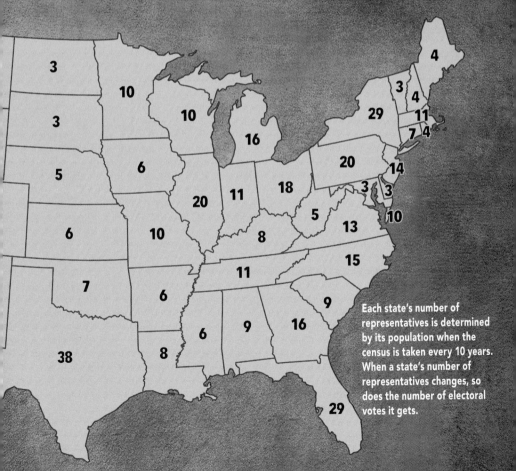

Each state's number of representatives is determined by its population when the census is taken every 10 years. When a state's number of representatives changes, so does the number of electoral votes it gets.

**ballot**—a piece of paper, or a card, used to vote in an election
**elector**—a person who votes to choose between two or more people running for office

# 270

the minimum number of electoral votes that a candidate needs to win the presidency. This number has varied through the years, based on the number of states and the number of members in the House of Representatives. But it's always equal to 50 percent of the total number of electors in the Electoral College plus one.

# 48

states and the District of Columbia follow a winner-takes-all rule. This means that whoever wins the majority of the popular vote receives all of that state's electoral votes.

# 2

states do not follow the winner-takes-all rule: Maine and Nebraska.

# 55

the most electoral votes of any state (California). Behind California:
**38** Texas
**29** Florida and New York
**20** Illinois and Pennsylvania

# 11

the fewest number of states a candidate could carry and still become president. Even if a candidate only won the states with the most electoral votes, he could still win the election.

55
16
29
20
20
18
14
20
15
16
38
29

# 3

the fewest number of electors a state may have. Each of these states has just 3: Alaska, Delaware, Montana, North Dakota, South Dakota, Vermont, and Wyoming. The District of Columbia also has 3 electors.

**3** number of times a president has won in the Electoral College despite having fewer popular votes than another candidate. This can happen because the winner-takes-all rule requires each elector of a state to vote for the winner of the popular vote in that state. Because some states have so many more electoral votes than others, it is possible to become president without winning the popular vote.

In the 2000 election, George W. Bush won with 271 electoral votes to Al Gore's 266. But Gore actually had about 500,000 more popular votes than Bush.

**ELECTORAL VOTE**     **POPULAR VOTE**

George W. Bush

**47.87%**

**271**

Al Gore

**48.38%**

**266**

**185-184**

Electoral College results in 1876. Samuel Tilden received about 250,000 more popular votes than Rutherford B. Hayes, but Hayes beat Tilden by one electoral vote.

**233-168**

Electoral College results in 1888. Grover Cleveland had about 90,000 more popular votes than Benjamin Harrison. However, Harrison beat Cleveland by a wide margin in electoral votes.

**1** number of times a person became president after coming in second in both popular votes and Electoral College votes. In 1824, Andrew Jackson secured about 40 percent of the votes in the popular election compared to 30 percent for John Quincy Adams. Two other candidates split the rest. When the Electoral College voted, all four candidates received votes. Jackson beat Adams 99 to 84 but 131 electoral votes were needed to win. Nobody had a majority of the electoral votes, so the House of Representatives decided who became president. They chose John Quincy Adams.

# CHAPTER 3

# WHAT NUMBER IS THAT AMENDMENT?

The U.S. Constitution sets out the rules for how our country should work. The Constitution was adopted in 1788, and there have been 27 **amendments** since then.

Each amendment changes something in the Constitution or tries to make its meaning clearer. A proposed amendment will only become part of the Constitution if three-fourths of all the states **ratify**, or agree, to it.

A number of constitutional amendments are related to presidential elections and the presidency.

**amendment**—a change made to a law or a legal document
**ratify**—to formally approve
**naturalize**—to give citizenship to someone who was born in another country

# 12th

This amendment slightly changed the process for how the Electoral College works. Originally, electors cast two votes for president. The person with the most votes became president and the runner-up became vice president. With the adoption of the 12th Amendment, electors must cast one vote for president and one for vice president. This reduces the chances that the president and vice president come from different political parties.

# 14th

This amendment said that all people who are born or **naturalized** in the United States are citizens of the United States and their home state. This 1868 amendment helped define what rights former slaves had, making it clear that they were also U.S. citizens.

# 15th

This amendment stated that neither the federal nor state governments may deny men the right to vote based on their "race, color, or previous condition of servitude [slavery]."

# 19th

This amendment, which was ratified in 1920, allowed all female citizens age 21 and older to vote.

# 20th

This amendment changed the date on which presidents are **inaugurated**. Presidents are now sworn in on January 20 rather than March 4 (unless the 20th is a Sunday). In the horse-and-buggy days, it took candidates that long to pack up and move to Washington, D.C. But by 1933, when the amendment was ratified, that was no longer an issue.

# 22nd

This amendment stated that a person may be elected as president no more than two times. If a vice president (or someone else in line for the presidency) ends up as president for more than two years, that person can only be elected once.

# 23rd

This amendment gave the District of Columbia three Electoral College votes. Until it was ratified in 1961, residents of Washington, D.C., could not vote in presidential elections.

# 24th

This amendment, which was ratified in 1964, made poll taxes illegal. A poll tax was a fee a voter had to pay before being allowed to vote. At the time, five southern states still charged a poll tax. The tax was intended to keep African-Americans from voting, but it affected anyone without the means to pay.

the inauguration of Barack Obama

# 25th

This amendment from 1967 outlined what happens if a president or vice president dies, resigns, or is otherwise unable to continue his duties.

*Give us liberty or give us death! PASS the 26th AMENDMENT*

# 26th

This 1971 amendment officially lowered the voting age from 21 to 18. Many people believed 18-year-olds should be able to vote because they could be **drafted** into the military.

## Who's Next?

In addition to the 25th Amendment, a law from 1947 determines what happens if both the president and the vice president die or are unable to serve.

18 people are in line for the presidency. This is called the order of **succession**:

- Vice President
- Speaker of the House of Representatives
- President pro tempore of the Senate

Next in line: The 15 heads of each **cabinet**, including:

Secretary of State
Secretary of the Treasury
Secretary of Defense
Attorney General

And so on down the line with the remaining cabinet officers. The order for succession is determined by the date the cabinet office was created. For example, the Department of Homeland Security was added most recently, so the head of it is last in line.

**inaugurate**—to swear an official into public office
**draft**—to be made to join the armed forces
**succession**—the order in which people replace someone who has left a position
**cabinet**—a group of officials who give advice to the president

# CHAPTER 4

# BIRTH OF A PRESIDENT

A president must be a natural born citizen, according to the Constitution. Anyone born in the United States is a natural born citizen. The phrase can also apply to someone born outside the country to American parents. It does not apply to someone who comes to the United States and takes steps to legally become a citizen.

**8** number of presidents born in America under British rule: George Washington, John Adams, Thomas Jefferson, James Madison, James Monroe, John Quincy Adams, Andrew Jackson, and William Henry Harrison. They were all born in North America before the United States became an independent nation.

**4** number of presidents born in hospitals rather than in the home: Jimmy Carter, Bill Clinton, George W. Bush, and Barack Obama

**7** number of presidents who had at least 9 siblings: George Washington, Thomas Jefferson, James Madison, James K. Polk, James Buchanan, Benjamin Harrison, and William H. Taft

**2** sets of fathers and sons have become president: John Adams and John Quincy Adams, and George H. W. Bush and George W. Bush.

George W. Bush (left) and his father George H. W. Bush

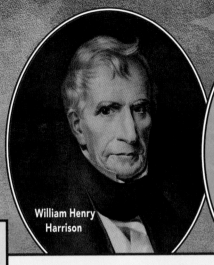

William Henry Harrison

Benjamin Harrison

**1** grandfather and grandson have become president: William Henry Harrison and Benjamin Harrison.

Theodore Roosevelt

Franklin Delano Roosevelt

**2** sets of presidents were cousins: James Madison and Zachary Taylor were second cousins. Theodore Roosevelt and Franklin Delano Roosevelt were fifth cousins.

FACT

Calvin Coolidge was the only president born on July 4, Independence Day.

# CHAPTER 5

# PRIOR EXPERIENCE

Nearly anything goes when it comes to a president's job history before taking office. Ronald Reagan was a well-known actor. Ulysses S. Grant and Dwight D. Eisenhower were military heroes. Jimmy Carter was a peanut farmer, governor, and navy officer. Grover Cleveland was a sheriff. But some career choices pop up more often than others.

Jimmy Carter on his peanut farm in Georgia.

RONALD REAGAN
ALEXIS SMITH
ZACHARY SCOTT
STALLION ROAD
WARNER PICTURE    JAMES V. KERN

Ronald Reagan appeared in 80 films before turning to a career in politics.

**7** number of presidents who served in the Civil War: Andrew Johnson, Ulysses S. Grant, Rutherford B. Hayes, James Garfield, Chester Arthur, Benjamin Harrison, and William McKinley

General Ulysses S. Grant

**7** number of presidents who served in World War II: Dwight D. Eisenhower, John F. Kennedy, Lyndon Johnson, Richard Nixon, Gerald Ford, Ronald Reagan, and George H. W. Bush

John F. Kennedy served in the U.S. Navy during World War II.

**28** number of presidents who have served in the military

General Eisenhower instructs his troops prior to the D-Day landing on June 6, 1944.

17

**15** number of presidents with no military service: John Adams, Thomas Jefferson, John Quincy Adams, Martin Van Buren, Millard Fillmore, Grover Cleveland, William H. Taft, Woodrow Wilson, Warren G. Harding, Calvin Coolidge, Herbert Hoover, Franklin D. Roosevelt, Bill Clinton, George W. Bush, and Barack Obama

Richard Nixon

Barack Obama

**26** number of presidents who were lawyers. Most of them went to law school. Others, such as Abraham Lincoln, studied on their own and worked in law offices. In addition to Lincoln, the lawyer presidents are: John Adams, Thomas Jefferson, James Monroe, John Quincy Adams, Andrew Jackson, Martin Van Buren, John Tyler, James K. Polk, Millard Fillmore, Franklin Pierce, James Buchanan, Rutherford B. Hayes, James Garfield, Chester Arthur, Grover Cleveland, Benjamin Harrison, William McKinley, William H. Taft, Woodrow Wilson, Calvin Coolidge, Franklin D. Roosevelt, Richard Nixon, Gerald Ford, Bill Clinton, and Barack Obama.

**19** number of presidents who served as governors before moving to the White House: Jefferson (Virginia), Monroe (Virginia), Van Buren (New York), William H. Harrison (Indiana Territory), Tyler (Virginia), Polk (Tennessee), Andrew Johnson (military governor of Tennessee during the Civil War), Hayes (Ohio), Cleveland (New York), McKinley (Ohio), Theodore Roosevelt (New York), Taft (governor-general of the Philippines), Wilson (New Jersey), Coolidge (Massachusetts), Franklin D. Roosevelt (New York), Carter (Georgia), Reagan (California), Clinton (Arkansas), and George W. Bush (Texas)

**14** number of men who served as vice president before taking the top job: John Adams, Jefferson, Van Buren, Tyler, Fillmore, Andrew Johnson, Arthur, Theodore Roosevelt, Coolidge, Harry Truman, Nixon, Lyndon Johnson, Ford, and George H. W. Bush

**6** number of presidents who previously served in the U.S. Senate

**9** number of presidents who previously served in the House of Representatives

**10** number of presidents who previously served in both houses of Congress

# 18

number of presidents who never served in Congress: Washington*, John Adams*, Jefferson*, Taylor, Grant, Arthur, Cleveland, Theodore Roosevelt, Taft, Wilson, Coolidge, Herbert Hoover, Franklin D. Roosevelt, Eisenhower, Carter, Reagan, Clinton, and George W. Bush
*served in the Continental Congress (before or during the Revolutionary War)

## FACT

Harry Truman loved music. As a child, he willingly got up at 5:00 a.m. to practice the piano. He often said he would have become a musician if he'd been good enough.

President Harry Truman shows off his talent as a piano player.

Abraham Lincoln obtained a patent in 1849. Patent number 6,469 was a device to help riverboats that got stuck on sandbars. No other president has ever obtained a patent.

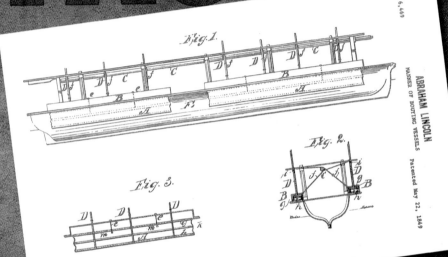

No. 6,469

ABRAHAM LINCOLN

MANNER OF BUOYING VESSELS

Patented May 22, 1849

Fig. 1.

Fig. 3.

Fig. 2.

**12** number of presidents without a college degree: Washington, Monroe, Jackson, Van Buren, William H. Harrison, Taylor, Fillmore, Lincoln, Andrew Johnson, Cleveland, McKinley, and Truman. Every president since Truman has had a college degree.

# CHAPTER 6

# WOMEN AND THE VOTE

Women in all states were guaranteed the right to vote when the 19th Amendment was ratified in 1920. They fought long and hard for more than seven decades for their right to **suffrage**.

Suffragist Elizabeth Cady Stanton speaks at the Senaca Falls Convention in New York.

# 11

number of proposals that won support at the first women's rights convention held in Seneca Falls, New York, in 1848. The ninth proposal, which stated that women should have the right to vote, passed only after much lively **debate**.

**suffrage**—the right to vote
**debate**—a polite discussion on something people disagree about

**$100**

amount of the fine imposed on **suffragist** Susan B. Anthony for voting in the 1872 election. She could have been sent to prison because she refused to pay the fine.

Susan B. Anthony was a leading figure in getting women the right to vote, but she was often shown as a troublemaker in the press.

**THE DAILY GRAPHIC**

*An Illustrated Evening Newspaper*

VOL. 1—NO. 81.  NEW YORK, THURSDAY, JUNE 5, 1873.  FIVE CENTS.

GRAPHIC STATUES, NO. 10.—"THE WOMAN WHO DARED."

**56**

number of individual state **referendums** that took place between 1867 and 1920 with the goal of permitting women to vote in those states.

**42**

years lapsed between the time a suffrage amendment was first introduced in Congress (1878) and when the amendment became law.

**suffragist**—one who works to get voting rights for those who do not have them
**referendum**—a public vote on an important issue

**0** number of presidents who publicly supported women's suffrage before Woodrow Wilson in 1918. In the 1912 election, Theodore Roosevelt's Progressive Party was in favor of voting rights for women, but Roosevelt lost the election.

**5,000** number of suffragists who participated in a parade in Washington, D.C., on March 3, 1913, the day before Wilson's **inauguration**. Hecklers injured 300 of the suffragists.

**11** number of states (out of 48) that had given women the right to vote by the 1916 presidential election: Arizona, California, Colorado, Idaho, Kansas, Montana, Nevada, Oregon, Utah, Washington, and Wyoming

**218**

number of women arrested in 1917 for peacefully picketing the White House to encourage President Wilson to support voting rights for women

**36**

number of states needed to ratify the 19th Amendment to give women the right to vote

**FACT**

In 1890 Wyoming was the first state to give women the right to vote.

**1**

vote made the difference. Tennessee was the 36th state to vote on ratification of the 19th Amendment. State representative Henry Burn was expected to vote against ratification. But when his suffragist mother sent him a note asking him to vote for it, he did. His vote made all the difference.

**inauguration**—a formal ceremony to swear a person into political office

# CHAPTER 7

# AFRICAN-AMERICANS AND THE VOTE

In theory, African-Americans were granted full citizenship rights in the years following the Civil War. The 13th, 14th, and 15th Amendments **abolished** slavery, recognized former slaves as citizens, and plainly said that they had the right to vote.

Reality was another story. For the next 100 years or more, many African-Americans were prevented from voting one way or another.

VOTE HERE
D THRU G

**23**

percent of **eligible** African-Americans were registered to vote prior to the Voting Rights Act of 1965.

**61**

percent of eligible African-Americans were registered to vote in the United States by 1969.

**59.8**

percent increase in the number of eligible African-American voters in Mississippi from 1965 to 1969

**abolish**—to officially put an end to something
**eligible**—qualified to participate

President Lyndon Johnson hands civil rights leader Martin Luther King Jr. the pen that he used to sign the Voting Rights Act into law.

Even after the 24th Amendment outlawed poll taxes in 1964, some states still tried to prevent African-Americans from voting. In 1965, President Lyndon Johnson signed the Voting Rights Act. It forbade states from using tests or other methods to keep people from voting.

# 219

years from Washington's election until a major political party nominated an African-American to run for president. Several candidates had competed in the **primaries**, including George Edwin Taylor in 1904 and Shirley Chisholm in 1972. But Barack Obama was the first to win his party's nomination to run for the top office.

**primary**—an election in which voters choose the party candidates who will run for office

# CHAPTER 8

# ELECTIONS AND ELECTION DAY

Originally, states could schedule Election Day any time within a 34-day window. In 1845, Congress chose the first Tuesday following the first Monday in November as Election Day.

Tuesday was chosen because many people had to travel long distances to get to the polls. Many wouldn't travel on Sunday because it was a religious day of rest. Wednesday wasn't a good choice either because it was market day in many rural communities.

## 3

number of states that didn't take part in the first election in 1789. Rhode Island and North Carolina hadn't yet ratified the Constitution. New York hadn't chosen electors for the Electoral College.

## 2

number of times a president has been elected unanimously. Both times it was George Washington. At that time, each elector cast votes for two different candidates. The candidate who received the most votes became president, and the runner-up became vice president.

**0**

number of times Zachary Taylor had voted before running for president

**0**

number of elected offices (other than during his school years) that Herbert Hoover held before becoming president

**900,000**

approximate number of votes cast in 1920 for Eugene Debs, the Socialist Party nominee. At the time, Debs was in prison for a speech he'd made against President Wilson and the entry into World War I. Debs finished third.

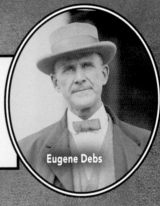

Eugene Debs

Harry Truman holds a copy of the Chicago newspaper that incorrectly reported his defeat.

**150,000**

number of *Chicago Daily Tribune* newspapers printed on Election Day 1948 with the headline, "Dewey Defeats Truman." The newspaper was so sure Thomas E. Dewey would win that it printed the paper before the polls closed.

**2,000,000**

approximate number of votes that Truman beat Dewey by in the 1948 popular election. Electoral College results: 303 (Truman) to 189 (Dewey).

# CHAPTER 9

# INAUGURATION:
## HAIL TO THE CHIEF

A president's first day on the job is Inauguration Day. On that day, the president promises to "preserve, protect, and defend the Constitution of the United States." Most of the time, Inauguration Day includes parades, balls, and parties. A few times, such as after an **assassination** or during times of war, the inauguration takes place without much celebration.

Barack and Michelle Obama dance at an inaugural ball to kick off his second term in office.

**135** number of words in George Washington's second inaugural speech. It is the shortest on record.

**737** number of words in the longest sentence from an inauguration speech (John Adams)

**8,468** number of words in William Henry Harrison's inauguration speech—the longest on record

**10** pounds. The weight of the Bible on which George Washington took his first oath of office. Presidents Harding, Eisenhower, Carter, and George H. W. Bush used this same Bible.

**2** number of presidents who were not married when elected. Grover Cleveland later got married at the White House. James Buchanan was a lifelong bachelor.

**assassination**—the murder of someone who is well known or important

**35** the age the Constitution states a president must be at the time of inauguration

**14** number of years that the president (and vice president) must have lived in the United States prior to inauguration

# 69 years, 349 days

Ronald Reagan's age at the time of his inauguration. He was the oldest president to take office.

# 42 years, 322 days

Theodore Roosevelt's age at the time of his inauguration. He was the youngest president inaugurated but not the youngest elected to the office. He was McKinley's vice president and became president when McKinley was assassinated.

# 43 years, 236 days

John F. Kennedy's age at the time of his inauguration. He was the youngest elected president to be inaugurated.

# CHAPTER 10

# PRESIDENTIAL PORTRAITS

The only common characteristic shared by all presidents, from Washington through Obama, is that each one has been male. These men have come in all shapes and sizes.

Hairstyles, facial hair, and clothing fashions have changed over the years. Prior to Andrew Jackson, presidents were always painted wearing knee breeches rather than pants. Our 23rd president, Benjamin Harrison, was the last president to have a beard.

Nearly **2** out of **3** presidents have claimed at least some English ancestry.

## 5 feet, 6 inches

height of three presidents: Martin Van Buren, Benjamin Harrison, and James Madison. However, many historians believe Madison was only 5 feet 4 inches tall, which would make him the shortest president.

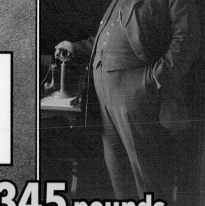

## 6 feet, 4 inches

height of Abraham Lincoln, our tallest president

## 345 pounds

reported weight of William H. Taft when he was inaugurated in 1909. He tried hard to lose weight and sometimes got down to 255 pounds.

# 100 pounds

approximate weight of James Madison, our lightest president

# 5

number of presidents who have their portrait on paper money that is currently being made: Washington ($1 bill), Jefferson ($2 bill), Lincoln ($5 bill), Jackson ($20 bill), and Grant ($50 bill)

# 4

number of presidential portraits that were on paper money that is no longer being made: McKinley ($500 bill), Cleveland ($1,000 bill), Madison ($5,000 bill), and Wilson ($100,000 bill)

# 6 gingers

These presidents all had various shades of red hair at some point: Jefferson, Van Buren, Hayes, Coolidge, Kennedy, and Carter.

# 7

left-handed presidents: Garfield, Truman, Ford, Reagan, George H. W. Bush, Clinton, and Obama

## FACT

About 1 in 10 people in the general population are left-handed. It is believed that Garfield and Ford could write with either hand. Other presidents may have been lefties as well, but because left-handedness was highly discouraged for years, there is no way to be certain. In the 1992 election, all three major candidates— Clinton, George H. W. Bush, and Ross Perot—were lefties.

# CHAPTER 11

# DEATH OF A PRESIDENT

On July 2, 1881, an assassin shot President Garfield. He lingered for more than two months. Doctors were unable to find the bullet in Garfield's body. They even tried using a metal detector—a recent invention of Alexander Graham Bell. No one realized that his bed had metal springs, which interfered with the machine.

No matter how it happens, the death of a sitting president sends the nation into mourning.

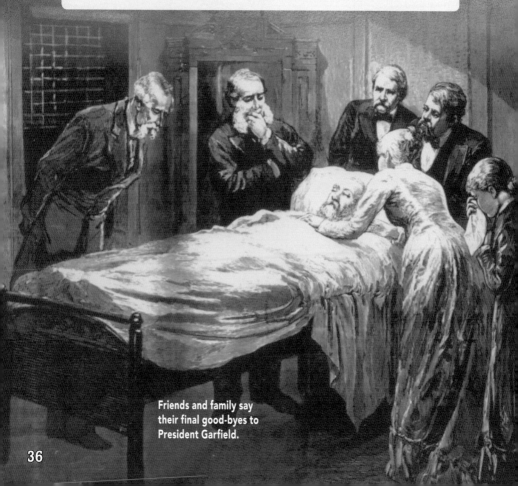

Friends and family say their final good-byes to President Garfield.

# 12 years, 39 days

length of Franklin D. Roosevelt's presidency, the longest

## 8

number of presidents who died in office: William Henry Harrison, Taylor, Lincoln, Garfield, McKinley, Harding, Franklin D. Roosevelt, and Kennedy

## 3

number of presidents who died on July 4. Both John Adams and Thomas Jefferson died on that day in 1826. Adams' last words were reported to be, "Thomas Jefferson still survives," but Jefferson had actually died earlier that day. James Monroe died on July 4, 1831.

## 4

number of presidents who were assassinated: Lincoln, Garfield, McKinley, and Kennedy

## 32 days

length of the shortest presidency. William Henry Harrison caught a severe cold at his inauguration on March 4, 1841. He did not wear a hat or coat despite the cold, rainy weather. His speech, which he delivered outdoors, lasted about 1 hour and 45 minutes.

## 120 years

length of the so-called 20-year curse. From 1840 to 1960, presidents elected every 20 years died in office: William Henry Harrison, Lincoln, Garfield, McKinley, Harding, Franklin D. Roosevelt, and Kennedy. Ronald Reagan, who was elected in 1980, was injured in an assassination attempt, but he recovered. This seems to have broken the curse.

# 1,000,000

estimated number of people who filed past Abraham Lincoln's open casket after his 1865 assassination. Some estimates say 1 out of 3 citizens came to pay respects as the funeral train passed by on its trip from Washington, D.C., to Springfield, Illinois.

# 23 years, 11 months

total amount of time vice presidents have served as president due to the death of the elected president

# 2,000

number of soldiers who accompanied Franklin D. Roosevelt's casket to the train station in Georgia (where he died) for the trip back to Washington, D.C.

Three-year-old JFK Jr. raises his arm in salute as his father's funeral procession goes by.

## 175 million

number of Americans estimated to have watched John F. Kennedy's funeral on television in 1963. Approximately a million more lined the streets to watch the funeral **procession** go by.

## 46 years, 178 days

age of the youngest president when he died: Kennedy

## 103 days

amount of time Polk lived after leaving office (just over 3 months)

## 93 years, 165 days

age of the oldest president when he died: Gerald Ford (after his presidency)

## 34 years and counting

Jimmy Carter has lived the longest after leaving office in 1981. The previous record was Herbert Hoover, who lived 31 years, 231 days after leaving office.

**procession**—a group of people walking or driving as part of a public festival, religious service, or parade

# CHAPTER 12

# VICE PRESIDENT WHO?

According to Article 1, Section 3 of the Constitution, the vice president's role is to serve as president of the Senate. There, the vice president casts any tie-breaking votes.

Unless they go on to become president, vice presidents' names are often forgotten after they leave office. Yet every vice president is just a heartbeat away from the most important job in the nation.

## 47
total number of vice presidents from 1789 to 2015

## 14
number of vice presidents who went on to become president

## 8
number of vice presidents who became president because the president died in office: Tyler, Fillmore, Andrew Johnson, Chester Arthur, Theodore Roosevelt, Coolidge, Truman, and Lyndon Johnson

Lyndon Johnson is sworn in as president shortly after the death of John F. Kennedy. Jackie Kennedy is by his side.

## 4
number of vice presidents who became commander in chief after the president died that were later elected president themselves: Theodore Roosevelt, Coolidge, Truman, and Lyndon Johnson

**1**

number of vice presidents who had a number one song. Charles Dawes, Coolidge's vice president, composed an instrumental tune in 1911. Words were finally written for the tune in 1951, and it was given the name "It's All in the Game." In 1958 it became a number one hit in the UK and the United States.

**7**

number of vice presidents who died in office: George Clinton (Madison), Elbridge Gerry (Madison), William King (Pierce), Henry Wilson (Grant), Thomas Hendricks (Cleveland), Garret Hobart (McKinley), and James Sherman (Taft)

**29**

number of tie-breaking votes John Adams cast in the Senate—a record among vice presidents

**3**

number of future vice presidents who signed the Declaration of Independence. Elbridge Gerry, Thomas Jefferson, and James Madison all went on to become vice presidents. Jefferson and Madison later served as commander in chief as well.

# 36 years, 1 month, 11 days

age of John Breckinridge on Inauguration Day. He was the youngest vice president.

## 1

number of vice presidents who later waged war against their own government. John Breckinridge served as vice president under James Buchanan (1857–1861). When the Civil War broke out, he volunteered for the Confederate army even though his home state, Kentucky, stayed with the Union. Mary Todd Lincoln, Abraham's wife, was his cousin.

# 71 years, 57 days

age of Alben Barkley, Harry Truman's vice president, on Inauguration Day in 1949. He was the oldest vice president.

## 1

number of vice presidents who took the oath of office outside the United States. William King, Franklin Pierce's vice president, had traveled to Cuba for health reasons. He was sworn in 20 days after Pierce's inauguration and died less than a month later.

## 1

number of times a vice president has defeated an **incumbent** president. In 1800 vice president Thomas Jefferson became president after defeating the sitting president, John Adams.

## FACT

Both of James Madison's vice presidents–George Clinton and Elbridge Gerry–died in office, one during each of Madison's two terms as president.

Gerald Ford (left) takes the oath of office in 1974. He is the only person to serve as president who was never nominated or elected to the office.

## 2

number of vice presidents who were **appointed**, not elected:

- In 1973, Gerald Ford was appointed vice president when Spiro Agnew resigned. A year later, he made history as the first appointed vice president to become president when Richard Nixon resigned.
- Nelson Rockefeller was appointed as Ford's vice president in 1974.

## $5,000

Vice President John Adams' salary in 1789. That would be more than $135,000 in today's money.

## $230,000

Vice President Joe Biden's salary in 2015

## FACT

The president and vice president travel separately to reduce the chance that both will be in an accident or the target of an attack.

**incumbent**—the current holder of an office
**appoint**—to choose someone for a job

# CHAPTER 13

# MAP IT OUT

WA

MT

ND

OR

ID

SD

WY

NV

UT

CO

NE
**Ford**

CA
**Nixon**

KS

AZ

NM

OK

**Eisenhower, TX**
**Lyndon Johnson**

**Obama**

HI

Has a president been born in your home state?
Check the map to find out.

Van Buren, Fillmore,
Theodore Roosevelt,
Franklin D. Roosevelt

Arthur, Coolidge

ME

VT

NH          Pierce

NY

MA

CT    RI

John Adams,
John Q. Adams,
Kennedy,
George H. W. Bush

George W. Bush

WI

MI

A

Hoover

IL

Reagan

IN

OH
Grant, Hayes,
Garfield, Benjamin
Harrison, McKinley,
Taft, Harding

PA
Buchanan

NJ

MD    DE

Cleveland

WV

VA

Washington, Jefferson,
Madison, Monroe,
William H. Harrison,
Tyler, Taylor, Wilson

MO

Truman

KT
Lincoln

NC

Polk, Andrew Johnson

TN

AR

Clinton

SC
Jackson

GA
Carter

MS

AL

LA

FL

# GLOSSARY

**abolish** (uh-BOL-ish)—to officially put an end to something

**amendment** (uh-MEND-muhnt)—a change made to a law or a legal document

**appoint** (uh-POINT)—to choose someone for a job

**assassination** (uh-sass-uh-NAY-shun)—the murder of someone who is well known or important

**ballot** (BAL-uht)—a piece of paper, or a card, used to vote in an election

**cabinet** (KA-buh-nit)—a group of officials who give advice to the president

**debate** (di-BATE)—a polite discussion on something people disagree about

**draft** (DRAFT)—to be made to join the armed forces

**elector** (ee-lehk-TOHR)—a person who votes to choose between two or more people running for office

**eligible** (EL-uh-juh-buhl)—qualified to participate

**inaugurate** (in-AW-gyuh-rate)—to swear an official into public office

**inauguration** (in-aw-gyuh-RAY-shuhn)—a formal ceremony to swear a person into political office

**incumbent** (in-KUM-bent)—the current holder of an office

**naturalize** (NACH-ur-uh-lize)—to give citizenship to someone who was born in another country

**nonconsecutive** (NON-kuhn-SEK-yuh-tiv)—with a gap between; not one after the other

**primary** (PRYE-mair-ee)—an election in which voters choose the party candidates who will run for office

**procession** (pruh-SESH-uhn)—a group of people walking or driving as part of a public festival, religious service, or parade

**ratify** (RAT-uh-fye)—to formally approve

**referendum** (rehf-er-EHN-duhm)—a public vote on an important issue

**succession** (suhk-SEH-shuhn)—the order in which people replace someone who has left a position

**suffrage** (SUHF-rij)—the right to vote

**suffragist** (SUHF-ri-jist)—one who works to get voting rights for those who do not have them

# READ MORE

**Bausum, Ann.** *Our Country's Presidents: All You Need to Know About the Presidents, From George Washington to Barack Obama.* Washington, D.C.: National Geographic Society, 2013.

**Davis, Todd.** *The New Big Book of U.S. Presidents.* Philadelphia: Running Press Kids, 2013.

**Halbert, Patricia A., ed.** *I Wish I Knew That: U.S. Presidents: Cool Stuff You Need to Know.* White Plains, N.Y.: Reader's Digest Assoc., 2012.

**Stabler, David.** *Kid Presidents: True Tales of Childhood from America's Presidents.* Philadelphia: Quirk Books, 2014.

# CRITICAL THINKING USING THE COMMON CORE

1. The 22nd Amendment limited the number of times a person could be elected president. This amendment was ratified in 1951, just six years after Franklin D. Roosevelt died during his fourth term as president. What are some reasons to limit a president's number of terms? (Integration of Knowledge and Ideas)

2. Compare and contrast the struggle for women's right to vote with the suffrage struggles of African-Americans. (Craft and Structure)

3. Because of how the Electoral College works, the candidate who wins the popular vote does not always become president. Do you think the Electoral College should be changed or kept as is? Use evidence from the text to support your answer. (Key Ideas and Details)

# INDEX

# INTERNET SITES

FactHound offers a safe, fun way to find Internet sites related to this book.
All of the sites on FactHound have been researched by our staff.

Here's all you do:
Visit *www.facthound.com*
Type in this code: 9781491482384